THE BIG BAND ERA

A NEW LOOK

Artie Shaw

THE
BIG BAND ERA

A NEW LOOK

BOB WILDER

Elderberry Press
OAKLAND

Elderberry Press, LLC
1720 Old Homestead Drive, Second floor
Oakland, Oregon 97462—9506.
E-MAIL: editor@elderberrypress.com
www.elderberrypress.com
TEL/FAX: 541.459.6043

All Elderberry books are available from your favorite bookstore, amazon.com, or from our 24 hour order line: (800) 431-1579

Library of Congress Control Number: 2002116077
Publisher's Catalog-in-Publication Data
The Big Band Era/Bob Wilder
ISBN 1-930859-52-X
1. Big Bands.
2. Jazz.
3. Benny Goodman.
4. Artie Shaw.
5. Jazz Vocalists.
I. Title

This book was written, printed, and bound in the United States of America.

This book is dedicated to my brother, Tom Wilder,
who knows more about the Big Band Era than anyone I know.

Chapter 1

The Big Band Picture

Anyone who had pep in his or her step during the 1930's and 1940's remembers well the Big Band Era. It was a time filled with rich memories of jukeboxes and jitterbugs that linger on in the hearts of those who danced their socks off and others who just stood in front of bandstands and listened to the energetic sound of joy.

It may be difficult for today's rock-indoctrinated CD buyers to understand it but, honestly, there was a time when you could actually understand the words to the songs that were being vocalized by boy and girl big band singers.

Anyone who memorized the lyrics to their favorite orchestrated ballads being played by any of the Big Five bands of the era—Tommy Dorsey, Benny Goodman, Harry James, Glenn Miller and Artie Shaw - will probably admit that it was while dancing cheek-to-cheek or what is known as touch-dancing nowadays. Sure it was corny moon and June and all that - but was it as bad as today's depressing moaning by a 14-year-old wearing braces over a lost love with a leather-wearing biker?

Well, let me tell you that in my time things were different because the Big Band Era was a huge, vibrating musical bazaar, a bubbling, exciting mixture of melodies, names of performers and the dancehalls and ballrooms which booked the big bands. It was and always will be remembered as the magnificent years of popular music and body-heat and whispering into your sweetheart's ear that you loved him or her. Wow, what a time, what a thrill.

If you were fortunate enough to live in one of the big band circuit cities, you could buy a theatre ticket to a Sunday matinee, which started at noon, for a few nickels and dimes. Sure, there were films, who remembers what was playing? No one. We were there for the big bands, the finger-snapping sounds of bands led by Woody Herman, Jimmy Dorsey or Shaw and - the cherry on the sundae - the crooning for Frank Sinatra or Perry Como.

And if you were extra flush - in the big bucks, so to speak—you could take your best girl dancing to a ballroom, where, say, someone like BG (Goodman) was playing.

Personally, I cannot think of how great the big band days were without reliving the memories of my days as an undergrad student at the University of Oklahoma, back in the 40's.

Dances at OU were the guys' favorite place to check out the chicks, to shake a leg to numbers like "Day by Day" and "It's a Blue World," sung by the Four Freshmen. And, in between cutting a rug, you could toss back a chilled bottle of 3.2 beer to cool down your libido. I also spent some time dancing in the girls' dorm at Pearl River Junior College (Miss.).

Big band buffs, like myself, like nothing better than to kick back and recall various jazz riffs being modified into swing arrangements - my kind of music.

There are some big band fans, to be sure, who can still immediately identify a jump tune like "Mission to Moscow" by BG after the first couple of notes. Not only that, they can also name the composer and, most definitely, the name of the arranger and swinging pianist, Mel Powell.

But big band buffs come in all flavors. Take my grandfather, for example. He would listen to the guitar-twanging, hot-fiddling tunes by Bob Wills and his Texas Playboys every day at noon on radio station KVOO in Tulsa, Okla. This was during the 30's and 40's, before that music was upgraded to Country and Western.

Wills' musicians were so good, let me remind you, that they could shift gears from the cowpie-kicking tunes into swinging big band arrangements.

It was a time when musicians, whether Nashville pickers or New York slickers, had their separate fan following. But if you danced to big bands regularly, it was no challenge to rattle off the names of who played lead trumpet for TD (T. Dorsey) or first sax for Miller.

It was a badge of honor for every sideman you could name in a band and although they're gone now, they are certainly not forgotten by anyone who ever did the Lindy Hop.

Chapter 2

The Real Peak

Big Band Era fanatics, such as I, still thrive as much on nonmusical nostalgia as on the appreciation of the spellbinding hit songs from the 30's and 40's, which, for me, pinpoint the best and most memorable years of pop music.

Among those with encyclopedic knowledge of the peak performances of pop music was George Simon, whose title was executive director of the National Academy of Recording Arts and Sciences.

Anyone with a love of big bands knows of and respects Simon's contributions to making sure we never forget. He crams a wealth of big band data into his fascinating book, "The Big Bands" (MacMillan, 1967).

Simon pinpoints the real peak of the Big Band Era as stretching from 1935 through 1946. It was a period, he points out accurately, when dance music was freshened by crosswinds that brought jazz and pop music together for the first and only time. It was a perfect blend of sound for listening and dancing and (dare I say it?) lovemaking.

This historical musical span - the Big Band Era - began with the rise of Benny Goodman in 1935 and his contribution or impact on the spread of swing band influence on the nation's social taste.

Goodman was given his big break when he was signed to play on a weekly Saturday night coast-to-coast radio program. He was popular, to a small regional degree, he thought. But, actually, his music was being appreciated in dancehalls and ballrooms everywhere in the nation, thanks to radio.

Goodman decided to book a cross-country tour, coast-to-coast, in July, 1935. But it was not what he expected. When his band got to Denver, Colo., he said, it was "just about the most humiliating experience of my life."

Even though he was a new musical treat, BG's orchestrations and style of dance music was not appreciated in Denver, where dancers started yelling for their money back. They wouldn't shut up until BG and his boys began playing waltzes.

Was that any way to treat a musical genius?

But it was all soon forgotten - well, almost - when the band reached Southern California for a series of appearances that ignited an inferno that would blaze into the big band craze.

So, there you have it. That started it. BG's band launched that decade - the 30's - with the sound of swing. And it would grow and grow and grow as armies of jitterbugs and bobbysoxers went into mesmerized musical meltdowns.

Chapter 3

Identity Means Style, Too

There were several reasons why Benny Goodman's music was so overwhelmingly popular and one of them was Fletcher Henderson, who was Goodman's arranger during the Big Band Era.

Henderson's contribution to the big band sound - the unison and the tempo or beat - was simply tremendous. He fronted his own band during the late 1920's and early 30's so he knew first-hand what to expect from the various musicians.

The breakaway big bands, the trend setters, established solid identities with their followers: The loyal radio listeners, the dancehall and ballroom dancers, and the record buyers. To sell those stacks of wax you needed more than just an immediately recognizable theme: You needed an individually identifiable style, too.

The manner in which big bands established their styles could be attributed to the sounds of Harry James' trumpeting on "The Mole" or Glenn Miller's trombone playing during "On a Little Street in Singapore." Or it could be the driving rhythm of Artie Shaw on just about anything, particularly "Any Old Time," accented by Billie Holiday's vocalizing, or the knee-slapping beat of Erskine Hawkins' big hit, "Tippin' In."

These were the numbers that had the hepcats jumpin'. Following the musical pace-setting arrangements by Henderson were the charts worked up by Sy Oliver, who was long associated with Tommy Dorsey's band.

Oliver had played trumpet - and he did it oh so well - for Jimmie Lunceford. It was Oliver's unique ability to arrange numbers with an emphasis on two instead of four beats to each measure.

One of Oliver's original arrangements, "Well, Git It!" (1942), pitted trumpeters Ziggy Elman and Chuck Peterson against each other and they never failed to bring down the house.

Among some of Oliver's other happy tunes were "On the Sunny Side of the Street," "Mandy!" and "Opus No. 1." These were all major hits and Oliver's enduring legacy was firmly established alongside of Henderson's musical gift.

As I reminisce about old bands and old tunes and old times, I cannot help but think about some of the interesting backgrounds of some of the old favorites. For example, Ted Weems originally recorded "Heartaches" in 1933, but nobody ever played it because the whistling of Elmo Tanner and the washboard rhythm background were not considered catchy enough.

It wasn't until 14 years later that a North Carolina radio disc jockey began playing "Heartaches" over and over and over that it caught on and became what was called an "overnight hit" in the music industry.

Chapter 4

The Big Band Picture

At one time or another, Tommy Dorsey's band featured such vocal talents as Frank Sinatra and Jo Stafford.

Sinatra, or "Oh, Frankie!" to the bobbysoxers, was with TD from 1940 through 1942. He earlier sang with Harry James for awhile. Stafford would also become a headliner on her own.

Other popular singers among my favorites were Connie Haines, Kay Starr, Betty

Hutton, Dinah Washington and Sarah Vaughn.

Along about the same time Marilyn Duke was singing with Vaughn Monroe, Kitty Kallen was with Jimmy Dorsey and James, and Anita O'Day was belting them out with Gene Krupa and Stan Kenton.

That O'Day, she was something else. There are few big band vocals that can compare with O'Day's "Let Me Off Uptown," "Boogie Blues," "That's What You Think" and "Knock Me a Kiss."

Doris Day, meanwhile, was perhaps the most famous female vocalist of the era because of the coast-to-coast radio exposure she got with Les Brown's band and the movies she eventually made. Note, I said she was probably the most famous, not the best, because Ella Fitzgerald was singing with Chick Webb and Peggy Lee was warbling with Benny Goodman's band.

If you've ever thought about the sometimes progression of a top arranger becoming a great band leader, well, it's only natural. Good examples of an arranger-turned-bandleader are Larry Clinton, Claude

Thornhill and Glenn Miller.

Miller, Clinton and Thornhill gradually shifted the dominant trend away from its original swing orientation, bringing the romantic ballad - a la Doris Day - back into the spotlight.

Bing Crosby preceded the Big Band Era, having broken into his crooning career with Paul Whitman's full-blown orchestra. A couple of other crooners who established themselves as popular dance band singers were Dick Haymes and Gordon MacRae.

Miller spearheaded the second phase of the Big Band Era, a time that was underscored by T. Dorsey's band when it was augmented by the dancehall-packing allure of Sinatra and the Pied Pipers, whose big hit was "Just as Though You Were Here."

Trumpter-leader James wanted strings with his band but he didn't have the funds to hire extra musicians. He got the cash finally when he signed with Columbia Records and the music lovers had James with strings.

You cannot think about the big bands without recalling some of their tribulations, the back-to-back one-nighters scattered all over a road map, cheap hotels, sleeping on buses, bad meals, gyp-artist dance promoters, and Saturday night dancehall gigs followed by Sunday afternoon matinees in movie houses.

There were enough headaches and heartaches to empty boxcars of aspirin and warehouses of booze, both good and bad, and then there were the personal tragedies that struck down some of the biggest names of the Big Band Era.

Miller was a major in the United States Army Air Force and directed the big AF band, which was exceptional, but he was killed in a plane crash while en route from England to France, Dec. 15, 1944. "American Patrol" and Miller were like ham and eggs.

Tommy Dorsey, a gambler and drinker, was another tragic story. He choked to death in his sleep in Greenwich, Conn., Nov. 26, 1956.

By contrast, Goodman defied the ravages of big band rigors and lived to a ripe old 75 before he died peacefully in his sleep Bon June 13, 1986. He was taking an afternoon nap before a night gig.

Davey Tough, an outstanding drummer in the 30's and 40's, died of injuries following a fall at a veteran's hospital on Dec. 6, 1948.

Hal McIntyre, who played tenor sax for Miller before fronting his own band, died in a California apartment fire on May 5, 1959.

And, in another shocking death, 20's and 30's band leader Ben Pollock hanged himself at his home in Palm Springs, Calif., June 7, 1971. He had been despondent over financial problems.

Meanwhile, frantic competition between bands and complex economic problems that plagued the leaders contributed to killing off big bands.

World War II was also blamed for the breakup of the big bands and changing the entertainment atmosphere of the nation.

Thousands of musicians were drafted, musical groups got smaller, and the musicians union's two-year ban on recordings shut down everything.

After WWII there was a surplus of bands. Then, unexpectedly, many of the big bands lost their boxoffice appeal when some of the most popular vocalists - Perry Como, Sinatra,

Haymes, Fitzgerald, Lee and Day - discovered they had the drawing power to break out on their own, and did just that.

George Simon said it all in his book with one sentence: "In December, 1946, almost a dozen years after Goodman had blown the first signs of life into the Big Band bubble, that bubble burst with a bang.

"Inside just a few weeks, the nation's top bands broke up: Benny Goodman, Woody Herman, Harry James, Tommy Dorsey, Les Brown, Jack Teagarden, Benny Carter and Ina Ray Hutton.

"All of a sudden, the magnificent years were all but over. The Big Band Era had ended."

Some of the big bands managed to stick around for a few more years, then folded.

Chapter 5

The Bands

Artie Shaw worked hard as a musician and bandleader and had more intellectual pursuits than the typical big band leader or musician.

Shaw liked to socialize . . . with socialites. He married several times. He began his musical career as a saxophone player and had added the clarinet to his instrumental expertise during his first job with Irving Aaronson.

He eventually organized his own group and

was a permanent fixture on the hit charts until he broke up his last big band in 1953. Two years later he stopped playing the clarinet altogether.

It was a popular debate of the day: Who was better on the clarinet, Goodman or Shaw?

Shaw became a giant big band celebrity in the 30's and 40's, leading varied and consistently excellent performing groups. You could accurately identify Shaw as a creative innovator and among the sounds he experimented with was the use of large string sections in his band during the 40's.

The ever artful Artie would outlive the other members of the "Big Five" band heroes: Benny Goodman, Tommy Dorsey, Harry James and Glenn Miller.

Another of my favorite top swing band leaders of the era was pianist Count Basie.

William "Bill" Basie organized his first band in 1935 in Kansas City, Mo., and by the end of the 30's had dancers swinging from coast-to-coast, especially when they punched "One 0' Clock Jump" on the juke box.

Big Band Era dancers had a wide range to pick their tempos from. There was swing

Latin and oh, yes, some Dixie, too. And the biggest Dixie hepcat was Bob Crosby, who started his Bobcats in 1935. But he was not born in Dixie. It was Spokane, Wash.

Whether being the brother of Bing was an asset or a liability is unknown but chances are it was a little of both.

Bob was handsomer than Bing and could sing, too. In fact, that was one of the negative things said about Bob's vocalizing: That he sounded too much like Bing.

Although brother Bob could croon, he was not a musician. He was a front man and an occasional vocalist and it worked just fine for him. He had his own following for many years.

Meanwhile, Les Brown was one of the big names who defied the demise of the Big Band Era. He was well known in the late 30's and into the new century, working steadily despite the decline of big band popularity.

Brown formed his first big group in 1938 and became a household name when he and his band began a long association with comedian Bob Hope in 1947.

Throughout his career, Brown consistently

fronted a top caliber organization with capable musicians.

There have been some feuds in musical circles but none rivaled the shouting and brawling that went on between the Brothers Dorsey, Tommy and Jimmy.

The Dorseys battled each other privately and in public. They seemed to have resolved their sibling and artistic differences in the spring of 1953 when they once again formed a single band. And they seemed to be on their way to becoming a big success as a team again when Fate intervened and they both died within a six-month period.

Tommy was the first to go when he choked to death in his sleep. Jimmy died of cancer the following year.

After co-directing the original Dorsey Brothers' Orchestra for more than a year, Tommy split to form his own band in 1935. His popularity was huge and extended into the early television years. He was one of the most dominating factors in big band circles for almost 20 years.

Tommy was a versatile performer on the trombone. He displayed a light swinging style as a studio musician early in his career and later concentrated on straight solo work and became famous for his smooth phrasing and beautiful tone. But he could break out with a rapid change of pace, evidenced by his work during the old ragtime standard, "Weary Blues."

It was Ralph Flanagan who supplied a grand flourish to the final days of the post-Big Band Era. His band was probably the No. 1 dance band in 1950 and was responsible for reigniting America's love affair with dancehalls and ballrooms.

Flanagan's plan was a revival of the Miller sound and it worked, too. He possessed top arranging skills and had a knack for recruiting superb musicians onto his bandstand. His music was a second wind during the fading days of big bands.

It was a glorious time for big band musicians - the 30's and 40's - and the King of Swing was Goodman (1909-86).

BG was a jazz giant and an all time great on the clarinet and it all began playing in a family band with his father. He formed his own band in the summer of 1934, debuting in Billy Rose's famous Music Hall.

Goodman's first band was a delayed sensation with a mid-1935 mediocre tour. But the band caught fire later that year in California while still on tour. His sensational rise to prominence in 1935 in considered by most musical historians as the single event that kicked off the Big Band Era.

BG became synonymous with swing and a great deal of the behind-scenes credit for the great BG beat must go to Fletcher Henderson, who was the first jazz artist to introduce the concept of "big band" divided into brass, reed and rhythm sections.

Beginning in 1934 and during the Big Band Era, Goodman was rocketing to fame as Henderson was writing his arrangements. It was a musical marriage between two perfectly matched talents.

One of Henderson's most memorable arrangements is "Down South Camp Meeting," which really swings.

Woody Herman also had great endurance as a bandleader. Herman was just a child when he began singing and playing and dancing in neighborhood shows in Milwaukee. He formed his first band in 1936 from remnants of the Isham Jones group, which featured Woody on clarinet and vocals for two years.

Woody's best effort singing and playing up front is "Laura," arranged by Ralph Burns.

It was in 1940 that Herman's future really began to brighten with the release of "Woodchopper's Ball." It has become a swing classic.

If anyone deserves a medal for his durability as a big band leader, it's Herman. He was in the business for more than half a century, working at his craft masterfully into the 1980's with a variety of "Thundering Herds."

Harry James was also around a long time. James played for more than three decades. He made his mark as a trumpeter with Goodman and went on to become highly successful on his own.

James admitted that his vigorous style was influenced by Louis Armstrong. Like Ol' Satch, James had great technique and a rich, brassy tone. He started his first band in 1939.

There was little doubt, right from the start, that James would become a musician. His father was the leader of a circus band and James' musical training began at a very early age. Conceivably the first Big Band Era musician raised in a circus, James made his debut with Ben Pollock's band in 1936.

James' career thrived during a residency of several decades in Las Vegas until his death from cancer in 1983. His wife, Betty Grable, was an actress and the No. 1 Pinup Girl during WWII.

On a personal note, I had the pleasure listening and dancing to James when he was at his finest. That was a very special night for me at the University of Oklahoma in 1947.

James was blowing his brains out that night, seeming to never leave the bandstand. I later found out that he was trying to atone for the night before. Some of my pals tipped me off that James was three sheets to the wind the night before and didn't spend much time on the bandstand.

There were some controversial big bands. Take Stan Kenton, for example.

Kenton's controversial-progressive jazz style of playing left no place for middle-of-the-roaders. His music, very difficult to dance to and designed more for listening, was either wholeheartedly endorsed or completely rejected.

Kenton worked for an assortment of bands as a piano player before starting his own band in 1941.

Three years later, Kenton's "Artistry in Rhythm" fixed his reputation as a distinctive voice in big band sounds. He died in 1979, following a series of mental health problems.

A drinker, Kenton once commented that one of the mental institutions in which he was a guest served a particular cocktail he had never before tasted: Clorox on the Rocks.

There were all types of showmen in front of some of the big bands. Few had more energy than Kay Kyser.

Kyser was big with his Kollege of Musical Knowledge presentations but he had a solid lineup of good musicians. Two of his vocalists, Harry Babbitt and Gloria Wood, were very popular.

Some of the big band leader's backgrounds never ceased to amuse or amaze the hepcats. Case in point: Jimmie Lunceford, a choirmaster's son who earned his bachelor's degree in music at Fisk University.

There were not many musicians with college diplomas tacked on their walls, believe me.

He was the leader of an outstanding, influential hot band in the 30's and 40's. His strength was appearances in ballrooms, theaters and colleges.

During a tour of the Pacific Northwest, Lunceford suffered a heart attack and died on July 1, 1947.

Miller's popularity remained constant for half a century after his death. Notably, his civilian band-leading career only spanned six years.

Miller established himself as a fine trombonist during his early years with bands fronted by Ben Pollock, Paul Ash and Red Nichols. His discovery of the distinctive sound obtained by combining clarinets with saxes is believed to have happened during his 1935-36 membership in British import Ray Noble's first American based band.

But when he went out on his own, Miller's first band, formed in 1937, failed to impress at box offices; however, his 1939 orchestra reached phenomenal heights with a number of music chart topping hits such as "Moonlight Serenade."

Miller joined the U.S. Army Air Corps after the outbreak of WWII and was soon leading a big band in the European war zone, entertaining troops until he vanished during a 1944 flight across the English Channel when he was only 40 years old.

The next big band I'd like to discuss is Vaughn Monroe's group, one of my all-time favorites. Monroe was one of the strongest boxoffice draws during the 40's and 50's.

Monroe was both a popular bandleader and vocalist.

He had a powerful baritone voice and had even studied for the opera at the Carnegie Tech School of Music. He broke into the band business as a trumpet player and organized his own band in 1940. His arrangements and sound were both excellent.

Monroe's first band in 1940 came up with the popular "There I Go," but he didn't achieve real big success until 1945 when his RCA Victor recording, "There, I've Said It Again," became a huge hit.

Sy Oliver came onto the big band scene as

a musician with Lunceford's group in the 30's and Tommy Dorsey's band in the 40's.

Oliver's arrangements were driven by a powerful two-beat style that produced an infectious sound and he absolutely ranks with Henderson as the most influential and imitated big band arrangers of all time.

An occasional leader of his own medium and large bands, starting in 1946, Oliver continued to influence the music industry as a freelance arranger. He often worked as a musical director for several record companies.

Another big band musician-leader who had a formal education in music was Claude Thornhill.

Thornhill received his musical education at the Cincinnati Conservatory and the University of Kentucky. His most successful years were when he was playing piano and leading a band in the 40's. His sensitive style of playing the piano and his subdued big band sound were a perfect blend for cheek-to-cheek dancers.

Thornhill would gain even more popularity during his association with Noble's orchestra during 1935-36 when he also did some of Noble's arrangements.

Before I leave a rundown of my favorite big bands I'd like to pay tribute to Texan Bob Wills, who recorded "Osage Stomp" and "Steel Guitar Rag," featuring Leon McAuliffe, in the 40's.

McAuliffe, also a Texan, was a whiz on the electric guitar, an instrument that took over the one-time fiddle-dominated Western swing band arrangements.

Hey, listen up. Do you hear that applause in the background? It's for all of the big bands. Maybe some of them were your favorites, too.

Chapter 6

Male Vocalists

Let's begin with the Eberle brothers, Ray and Bob.

Ray Eberle's voice was pitched slightly higher than Bob's and that melodious pitch was tailor-made for Miller's muted brass and reeds.

But Bob was a star in his own right, just as the Brothers Crosby, Bing and Bob, had their own identities.

Harry Babbitt was a baritone with a smooth, silken quality and was big with the

Kay Kyser band in the late 30's and early 40's.

Nat "King" Cole, one of the best of the best, started out as a jazz pianist. Cole was such a good pianist that he could have become a superstar just playing piano if he had never sung a note in his life.

Cole was a leading pop singer of the 40's and 50's. Some of his best records are still being played on the radio today, especially "Mona Lisa" and "Walking My Baby Back Home."

Dick Haymes was another giant among the best pop singers during the 40's and 50's. He was married several times and among his wives was Rita Hayworth.

But Haymes was plagued by a gambling addiction and it kept him in serious debt in places like Las Vegas.

Haymes, who had a rich baritone voice, was hired by James in early 1940. He attained prominence in just one year, one of his biggest hits being "My Silent Love," then switched to Goodman's group during March-July, 1942.

Among the other big band vocalists were Vic Damone, who like Haymes made some movies, and Harry Prime, an excellent vocalist with Randy Brooks, Jack Fina, Ralph Flanagan and Tommy Dorsey during the 40's and 50's.

Prime recorded "Until" with Dorsey and "I Should Care" with Flanagan,

And don't forget Mel Torme, "The Velvet Fog." Torme was a juvenile lead in a lot of movies and, like Mickey Rooney, was expert on the drums.

Torme was a versatile performer in front of small trios or big orchestras, in recording studios, on TV specials, during one man shows and jazz concerts. He also was an accomplished piano player, composer, arranger and even wrote a couple of books. And could he swing.

One of my other favorite up-beat swingers was Louis Jordan of "Is You Is Or Is You Ain't My Baby?" fame.

Jordan wailed on alto sax and did a lot of his bebop jump band's vocals, such as "GI Jive," "Caldonia," "Choo Choo Chi Boogie" and "Ain't Nobody Here But Us Chickens."

I had the pleasure of meeting Jordan during a gig he was playing in Stockton, Calif.

He told me a lot of entertaining things about his life and career as a musician.

Jordan was a good showman and early reached the top of the pop record charts with his seemingly unlimited energy and enthusiasm for music.

If anyone could make a joint jump, it was Jordan. Oh, yeah!

Chapter 7

Female Vocalists

Helen Forrest, without a doubt, was the outstanding female vocalist of the 30's and 40's.

Her voice was strong if not powerful while singing songs of love, romance and plain old happiness.

Forrest had a warm voice that could make you believe in the words and meaning of a song. She had musical sensitivity and a fine ear for subtle nuances.

Take a record like "It's Always You," which she made while she was with Benny Goodman. Arranged by Eddie Sauter, "It's Always You" showcases her at her best.

I had the pleasure of chatting with Miss Forrest in the 70's one night when she was booked into Stockton. We talked at length while sipping adult beverages. She recalled some of her experiences with the Shaw, Goodman and James bands in the 30's and 40's.

I also admired Kitty Kallen. One of her best numbers, in my opinion, was "I'm Beginning To See The Light," which she cut while she was with James. She was outstanding with both bands and later on as a single performing artist.

Kallen was definitely one of the bright lights of the Big Band Era.

Another upfront singer, during the 40's and 50's, was Vera Lynn, who was born in London. She sang with a strong plaintive voice and was a pleasure to listen to, especially on her 1949 hit, "Again."

And if it was husky-throated singing from a female you wanted, Anita O'Day certainly filled the bill.

O'Day's clear lyrics and upbeat phrasing established a trend among the female singers of her day. She could belt out a ballad or a torch song.

A million dollar talent, Miss O'Day admittedly fouled-up her career with harmful choices in her personal life. She did it all and made no apologies.

Gene Krupa and Kenton were driving forces when it came to pulse-pounding music and O'Day was a perfect figurehead for their musical ships.

My favorite O'Day rendition? That's easy, it's "Massachusetts," which she cut when she was with Krupa.

Jo Stafford and her sisters formed a family trio when they were young in Coalinga, Calif., where she was born. The family trio started harmonizing with a couple of boys' groups in 1938 when 20th Century Fox Studios brought in some top vocal groups for the film, "Alexander's Ragtime Band."

The quasi "big" band sound of the harmonizing groups, who called themselves the Pied Pipers, started drawing some attention and the rest is history.

Jo Stafford was leading a Pied Piper quartet in 1939 when they hooked up with Tommy Dorsey.

Paul Weston, who had been Dorsey's arranger since 1935, and Stafford became very close friends away from the bandstand and when he left Dorsey he stayed in touch with her. Their paths would cross again at Capitol Records and they were married.

And anyone who remembers the Hit Parade cannot help but think of Bea Wain, who broke in with Larry Clinton in the 30's.

Wain, who had a warm, melodious delivery, was with the Hit Parade off and on from 1939 until mid-1941. She left Clinton's band in 1939 to work as a single.

There's no doubt about it: I had a crush on the New York City-born songbird and I still treasure her work on tapes and CD's.

If I had to name the two quintessential Big Band Era female vocalists they would be Helen Forrest and Helen Ward.

Ward was only 18 when Goodman hired her in 1934. She had a straightforward style with a strong sense of rhythm. She stayed with BG for two years.

Although she was retired between 1937 and 1942, except for a few recording sessions, she returned to the bandstand with Hal McIntyre in 1943, and was with James briefly in 1944.

Fran Warren was another excellent pop vocalist. The essence of her great singing style derived directly from Ivie Anderson, who sang with the Duke Ellington orchestra.

Warren's big hits were "Sunday Kind of Love" and "Early Autumn" with Claude Thornhill's band.

Anderson's interpretation of "I've Got It Bad (And That Ain't Good)" is perhaps the most memorable of the sides she cut when she was with the Duke.

And then there was Margaret Whiting, who was the daughter of noted composer Richard Whiting.

Miss Whiting's biggest hits were "My Ideal" and "Moonlight in Vermont."

Anyone who hasn't heard "Moonlight in Vermont," backed by Billy Butterfield's band, just hasn't heard big band singing. Right?

Chapter 8

Vocal Groups

When you start talking about vocal groups, either all-boy, all-girl or mixed boys and girls, you must begin with the Modernaires from the Glenn Miller years.

Among the Modernaires' biggest hits were "Juke Box Saturday Night," "I Got a Gal in Kalamazoo" and "Chattanooga Choo Choo."

These were the type of tunes that you played in the jukebox for a nickel and then sang the lyrics along with Paula Kelly or

Marian Hutton, who sang lead for the group at different times.

"Chattanooga Choo Choo" sold a million copies during the first six months of its release in 1942.

Everywhere you went, civilians and servicemen were humming, singing or whistling along to the sound of "Chattanooga Choo Choo" and disc jockeys couldn't spin it often enough on the radio shows.

The Pied Pipers of the Tommy Dorsey era were also among the best of the vocal groups. Why not? They backed Frank Sinatra on a number of his recordings. And they could really sing and swing together.

There were seven Pipers to begin with - all males. Then Jo Stafford came along and the group's appeal improved enormously with its manner of harmonizing romantic ballads and slow-paced mood numbers.

Excellent harmonizing combined with good phrasing were the strong points of the Pied Pipers' appeal.

Two more of my favorite groups were the Four Freshmen, formed in 1948, while members were attending the Arthur Jordan Conservatory of Music in Indianapolis.

The Four Freshmen lent an innovative sound to recording groups and caught on with the record-buying public immediately. They were big hits on college big band dance dates.

Tommy Dorsey also signed the Clark Sisters, a trio that contributed to the superb version of "On the Sunny Side of the Street."

Chapter 9

Recordings

It's time to talk records.

I'm going to discuss about 100 records, selected from the many thousands that were cut during the Big Band years, spanning the middle 30's into the early 50's.

Let's begin with Frank Sinatra's "There's No You." Frank is backed by Axel Stordahl's studio band in 1945. This platter, in my estimation, is the finest ballad of all time. However, it never got to be very popular. But, remember, that was early Sinatra.

On the record Sinatra is saying, in essence, something that many lovers realize: They know the affair was never meant to be.

Vera Lynn recorded "Again" and it is a haunting refrain, made unforgettable by the gifted English songbird when she sings "Again, this doesn't happen again. We'll have this moment forever, but never, never again."

It was obvious that Harry James had discovered a major singing and musical talent in Sinatra, whose presence had a more than casual impact on the James band's popularity.

Sinatra's original way with a phrase can be heard in "All or Nothing At All," cut with James' band in 1939. A moderate success at first, "All or Nothing At All" became a big hit when it was re-released a few years later, proving that timing is everything.

Artie Shaw's clarinet work was always smooth and doubly pleasurable when coupled with Helen Forrest. Together they made romantic ballads that encouraged close dancing in dimly lighted dancehalls.

Stirring up the high school and college

dance crowds in the mid-40s was Anita O'Day's "And Her Tears Flowed Like Wine," backed by Stan Kenton.

Kenton's arrangement, with drummer Jesse Price providing the loosely swinging beat, was accurately designed for O'Day's distinctive delivery. The 1944 recording became a major hit, Kenton's first.

But the record that established Kenton as a solid big band force for all time was his theme song, "Artistry in Rhythm," which originated from a passage in Ravel's ballet, Daphnis of Chloe.

"Artistry in Rhythm" - This fast moving arrangement became a major success - yes, a million record hit.

Now that you've caught on to what I'm up to, let's continue the beat with these selections:

"Atlanta, Ga." - This well-arranged 1945 goodie by the Woody Herman band features Woody on the vocal and is an interesting blend of band power and blues. Herman tosses in a great clarinet solo which complements his relaxed singing style. It's a lively, feel-good tune that will help you lose the blues.

"Baby Face" - This was a smash hit for Jan Garber's orchestra in 1926 but Art Mooney revived the old hit in 1948. That same year Mooney turned out "I'm Looking Over a Four-Leaf Clover," another big seller.

"Back Beat Boogie" - A superb trumpet soloist like James certainly energizes swinging tunes like this one.

"Beg Your Pardon" - Top-notch piano work by bandleader Francis Craig and vocal by Bob Lamm, this one came out of nowhere, caught on and became a big hit, following Craig's 1948 hit, "Near You." An interesting transformation of classical material.

"Blue Moon" - Monroe put his vocal talents to good use on this number and it sold well, just like most of his band's recordings.

"Bugle Call Rag" - Miller drummer

Maurice "Moe" Purtill's fine work makes this one really jump. Purtill contributed mightily to Miller's success because the most critical player in the rhythm section is the drummer with his sharply etched backgrounds.

"Call Me Devil May Care" - A combination of one of Dorsey's best arrangements and a Sinatra vocal, this one's a winner out of the gate.

"Caribbean Clipper" - A typically really, great Miller swinger that the jitterbugs really enjoyed. The side featured Tex Beneke on the alto sax.

"Cherry" - The strings on this rendition go well with James' horn. The slow pace was easy for the foxtrotters and is remembered as one of the first popular sides by James' band.

"Darktown Strutter's Ball" - Goodman comes up with a perfect swing arrangement, filled with plenty of delights and some rather exceptional solos.

"Day by Day" - There is plenty of zing to go with this top-notch arrangement by what I consider to be the best vocal group during the Big Band Era— The Four Freshmen.

"Dream" - The Pied Pipers do justice to Johnny Mercer's lyrics, which made this the No. 2 song for the Pipers in 1945. Whenever anyone said so long to a sweetheart in '45, it was probably after dancing cheek-to-cheek to this one.

"Eager Beaver" - Kenton's revolutionary progressive jazz style of arranging brought a new sound to Big Band enthusiasts in 1943. He recorded "Eager Beaver" in '43 and it features a great piano introduction by Kenton before the swinging, brassy band takes command. As always, excitement prevails when Kenton is at the keys.

"Early Autumn" - The band is Claude Thornhill's and the vocal is by Fran Warren, who was able to drop her otherwise ever-present Bronx accent when she sang.

"Easy to Love" - A straight up-and-down dancer's delight by Shaw's versatile group. It's one of his best arrangements.

"Hot Toddy" - Showcases a lively, swinging sound by Flanagan's bandstand troops.

"How Blue the Night" - Dick Haymes, as always, is masterful in his phrasing.

"I Dream of You" - The Dorseys get it together with Tommy on trombone and Jimmy on the sax. What a combo.

"Gotta Be This or That" - Although he is not credited, BG fanatics can detect his vocalizing, such as it is, and his peerless clarinet playing is at its best. This one climbed to No. 2 in 1945, thanks to some enhancing bass-slapping by Slam Stewart.

"I Dreamt I Dwelt in Harlem" - Johnny Best on trumpet and Beneke on sax are featured on this jump tune, which, to my surprise, never become very popular. The band was obviously having a great time.

"I Guess I'll Have to Dream the Rest" - This low-paced mood ballad, with Dorsey's band backing Sinatra and the Pied Pipers, hits a home run.

"I Hear a Rhapsody" - This 1941 record is one of the all time greatest. How could it go wrong with Forrest's singing and BG's uniquely innovative arrangement? Brings back memories of my school days.

"I Heard You Cried Last Night" - James' long trumpet solo sets the mood for this romantic instrumental.

"I'm in the Mood for Love" - Recorded by an unknown studio band, but the arrangement is first class and, to me, sounds a lot like Nelson Riddle in his moonlighting phase.

"I'm Looking Over a Four-Leaf Clover" - It was nostalgia time when this grand old tune was revived by Mooney's band. A catchy arrangement features a lively vocal group. Mooney specialized in sing-along versions of old-time songs. This tune was first popular in 1927 and Mooney revised it in 1948.

"Invitation" - This one by Les Brown's band barely made the radar screen. Too bad it wasn't more popular because it has a haunting melody with a near-perfect arrangement.

"I Only Have Eyes for You" - This one is a mystery arrangement of a recording that is one of the best renditions of a Big Band Era song. The arrangement is done in Miller's style, featuring a clarinet lead.

"I Should Care" - This is one of the best foxtrot dance step numbers ever recorded. The solos by the Dorseys are unforgettable. It was cut after they got back together - if only briefly before they both died.

Harry Prime also sang "I Should Care" with Flanagan's orchestra. He was backed by the Singing Winds. The result was a good romantic ballad with one of the better arrangements of the day.

"Is You Is or Is You Ain't (My Baby)" -

This is probably Louis Jordan's first Tympany Five side. The song, on the flip side of "G.I. Jive", was co-written by Billy Austin and Jordan. In fact, it surpassed "G.I. Jive" and reached No. I on the hit charts. Jordan would have 16 more hits within the next five years. He kept the jukeboxes in malt shops going night and day.

"It's a Blue World" - This is a sad song with a slow tempo but with the Four Freshmen vocalizing it never drags.

"It's Always You" - Forrest and Goodman. Simply dynamite, especially with Eddie Sauter's innovative arrangement. One of my favorite recordings, it was cut in 1941. Sauter's flawless arrangement showcased Forrest's talent to the finest degree.

"I've Got You Under My Skin" - A memorable ballad that swings. And why not? It's Sinatra backed by Count Basie's band. A typical Chairman of the Board smash.

"I've Had This Feeling Before" - James'

dramatic arrangement with strings provides a nice contrast to Helen Ward's sexy vocalizing. Cut in 1944, this one personifies the Big Band Era sound.

"I Wish I Didn't Love You So" - This big hit by Monroe came out of the 1947 Betty Hutton movie, "Perils of Pauline." Most of Monroe's arrangements were underrated, but not this time as he's solidly backed by the Moon Maids. Vaughn's simply great as lead vocalist.

"I Wish I Knew" - Another good example of Dick Haymes' excellent vocalizing. This one came out of the 20th Century Fox film, "Diamond Horseshoe."

"Jingle, Jangle, Jingle" - Where did Kay Kyser find all of those good girl singers? Julie Conway and The Group join in with Harry Babbitt on this lively, offbeat 1942 recording that just about everyone who ever heard it enjoyed. It was from a movie, "Forest Rangers," starring Fred MacMurray and Susan Hayward.

"Laura" - This classic, done by Woody Herman's Herd with Woody on the vocal, was made in 1945. It's a classic song that helps you recall your first - but not forgotten - love. Woody backs himself with a sax solo. It came from the 1945 film, "Laura," with music by Dave Raksin and haunting lyrics by Johnny Mercer. It became a gold record for Herman's band.

"Let's get lost"- The 4 Lee Sisters back Monroe on this 1942 recording. Vaughn pleads, "Let's Get Lost" and one of the 4 Lee Sisters replies sexily, "Well, should we?" It's a top arrangement with great drum work. On that same recording date Monroe cut "Hip, Hip Hooray" with vocalizing by the 4 Vees and "Happy Go Lucky" with Marilyn Duke doing the honors. Both sides got favorable reaction.

"Let Me Off Uptown" - This is a slamming arrangement and vocal, featuring one of the greatest swing drummers of all, Gene Krupa, and a really hep singer, Anita O'Day. Jazz innovator Anita was never better. Together they were electricity, energy and excitement unleashed. Throw in Roy Eldridge's spine-tingling trumpet solo and, well, you've got swinging perfection. Roy stops the show when Anita prompts him to "Blow, Roy, Blow!"

"Little White Lies" - This one was a big success for Haymes, who revealed that he had a bad cold when he recorded it. In fact, he was quoted, "I didn't think this record would make it. I didn't even like it." Well, he obviously had good help from Gordon Jenkins' orchestra and some vocalizing backup work by the Four Hits and a Miss. How wrong could anyone be?

"Mam'selle" - Underrated Art Lund (real name Art London) does a very good job on what became a big hit for him. He had been with Goodman at one time. The song was originally heard in a movie, "The Razor's Edge," with Tyrone Power, Gene Tierney and Clifton Webb.

"Mandy!" - It's Tommy Dorsey's band with trumpeter Ziggy Elman and drummer Buddy Rich hammering out a beat that can't be beat.

"Massachusetts" - Here we go again, Krupa and O'Day, with energy and enthusiasm to spare. O'Day's diction and articulation are simply superb.

"Mission to Moscow" - Goodman is going wild on the clarinet and the sax section is shining with arranger Mel Powell providing some excellent support on the piano. The strings and jazz instruments co-exist extremely well on this smartly charted arrangement. Powell also arranged for Miller's U.S. Army Air Force Band.

"Moonlight in Vermont" - Trumpeter Billy Butterfield is the star of this ballad, which features Margaret Whiting on vocal.

"My Devotion" - Like most of Monroe's singing, this one is very easy to listen to and dance the night away.

"My Heart Stood Still" - The upbeat tempo of this Shaw selection, usually played in a slow dance mode, comes off with a perfect fast beat for dancers, who have no trouble swinging to some great trumpet work.

"My Heart Tells Me" - This was one of Glenn Gray's last hits and features vocalist Eugenie Baird in a smooth, straightforward but emotional performance. The song was featured in the film, "Sweet Rosie O'Grady," starring Betty Grable.

"Night and Day" - Goodman provides a faster than usual arrangement for this song that was also recorded by Dorsey. But it was a refreshing break to hear BG's version. Dorsey's arranger, probably Paul Weston, livened it up with one of the most clever arrangements of the Big Band Era. Foxtrot or swing, take your choice.

"Oh, Look at Me Now" - Surprisingly, Connie Haines and Sinatra team up on this novelty number with T. Dorsey's band. But it just goes to prove that Sinatra could handle any type of song.

"On a Little Street in Singapore" - One of Miller's best arrangements features Ray Eberle on the vocal. The ballad is clear and precise, satisfying and memorable.

"On a Slow Boat to China" - This record, featuring vocalists Babbitt and Gloria Wood, was Kay Kyser's final appearance on the hit charts. It starts slowly with Babbit's vocalizing, then picks up when perky Wood joins in.

"Osage Stomp" - Without a doubt, I think this fast-paced zinger by Bob Wills is the best Western swing recording of all time.

"Out of Nowhere" - Typical Les Brown arranging - superb and perfectly executed. Features a wonderfully crafted trumpet solo by Billy Butterfield.

"Penthouse Serenade" - Flanagan's orchestra makes great use of Miller's clarinet-led reed section plan and the "boo-wah" phrasing of the trumpets comes close to Miller's style.

"It's Always You" — Benny Goodman's fine clarinet leads the listener into Forrest's stirring vocal. It's another great Sauter arrangement, original and exciting. Following Forrest's vocalizing, BG's closing bars are something else.

"Rag Mop" - A typically outstanding Flanagan arrangement, featuring a great drum solo, this recording was a spirited jump tune out of the Korean War years.

"Red Bank Boogie" - No question, this is Basie's best, and features Buck Clayton on trumpet.

"Rainbow Rhapsody" - This one's nice to dance to, a slow instrumental that even mediocre foxtrot enthusiasts can handle.

"Say It" - T. Dorsey and Sinatra in 1940. Oh, so smooth.

"September Song" - Brings back memories of 1945 and the end of WWII. A slow Artie Shaw piece with no vocal, which is not necessary for a touch of nostalgia. Roy Coniff was the arranger and he provided a fresh orchestration.

"Serenade to a Savage" - One of Shaw's standards that has held up through the years. Swinging hepcats really cut a rug to this 1943 arrangement.

"Six Flats Unfurnished" - The arrangement is by Fetcher Henderson for BG's swinging group.

"Sleepy Lagoon" - It is the summer of 1942 and Harry James' horn solo is perfect and never fails to bring back WWII memories by those who were either on the homefront or in the military.

"Somebody Else Is Taking My Place" - Who doesn't like BG and Peggy Lee on this type of song? This 1942 disc is Lee's biggest with Goodman. Like the clarinet? The arrangement is, of course, top notch.

"Something Sentimental" - A typical Monroe effort. His arrangement and his vocal. Both are excellent.

"South Rampart Street Parade" - It's Yank Lawson on trumpet leading Bob Crosby's Bobcats on this spectacularly exciting recording.

"Speak Low" - This is usually a slow-dance instrumental but Brown adds some spice to the dance recipe, much to the joy of the swingers.

"Stardust" - Who could ever top Shaw's arrangement? Some experts claim Lennie Hayton's arrangement is just about perfect and what about Jack Jenny's trombone solo? Memorable, to say the least. "The extraordinary octave leap by Jenny to High F was admired by sophisticated audiences," writes Gunther Schuller in Swing Era, "not only from the ease with which he managed the deal, but for his elegance and sensitivity of phrasing."

"Steel Guitar Rag" - The gusto on steel guitar on this Bob Wills' floor-stomper is provided by Leon McAuliffe. Wills had turned more and more to a jazz repertory and instrumentation, adding trumpets and saxes.

"Sun Valley Jump" - This one, in contrast to a typical Miller ballad, really jumps.

"Tampico" - It's a novelty song with a sense of irony a la Andrews Sisters but with June Christy belting out the lyrics, it sold one million records - Kenton's first appearance in that charmed circle. Originally written for Anita O'Day before she quit Kenton's band, Christy pays tribute to O'Day's style. Makes you remember 1945 for something besides WWII.

"There Are Such Things" - Let's see now: TD, Sinatra and the Pied Pipers. Is that a formula for success or what? It's one of the great love ballads, No. 1, by far, on everyone's hit parade. Sinatra is at his best on this 1942 side and Dorsey's trombone solo is peerless, as usual, with strings providing the background support.

"There, I've Said It Again" - The arrangement, in slow key, is a big plus behind Monroe's vocalizing. The one made every romantic's heart beat a little bit faster in 1945.

"There'll Be Some Changes Made" - The sexy, sultry vocal on this BG record is by Louise Tobin. There is some fine work by the sax section to go with BG on the clarinet and Henderson, who did the arrangement, chips in some solid piano backing. And that's James on the trumpet solo. He and Tobin were married at the time. The song was originally made famous by Ethel Waters of stage and film fame in 1922.

"These Things You Left Me" - Goodman's clarinet backing of a Forrest vocal were simply not lacking for anything but, go figure, it never got that popular.

"This Is Always" - Buddy DeVito does the vocal on this James record. It's a fine band backup to a good ballad by an underrated singer.

"This Love Of Mine" - T. Dorsey plus Sinatra equals a million-plus hit on the juke-boxes. The style of rendition was imitated by other singers and vocal groups in years to come. The abnormally slow tempo on the record is carried off well by Sinatra, who always had an exceptional sense of musical savvy.

"Trolley Song" - Oh, yes, it's from the movie, "Meet Me In St. Louis." Stafford and the Pied Pipers are backed by Paul Weston's studio band in a splendid arrangement. Cut in 1944, the number reached No. 2 on the charts for awhile.

"True" - Monroe's band plus vocals by Monroe and the 4 Lee Sisters, in my opinion, makes this ballad one of the best of all Big Band Era records. It's the ultimate foxtrot piece with a super arrangement.

"Trumpet Blues" - This fast instrumental, almost too fast for the jitterbugs, was underrated.

"Twelfth Street Rag" - A Dixieland toe-tapper by Pee Wee Hunt that made everybody sit up and take notice. Hunt was a trombonist for Glen Gray and his Casa Loma Orchestra for 14 years before breaking out on his own.

"Ultra" - This exciting arrangement by James jumps but it never got the credit it deserved. The instrumental arrangement really swings and builds. One of James' best efforts.

"Until" - Harry Prime, the Clark Sisters and the Town Criers give T. Dorsey his money's worth. This beauty, recorded in 1949, melded a nice slow arrangement with the vocalists. And Mr. T gets an ovation for some great solo work on the trombone.

"Waiting For the Train To Come In" - You

can feel the anxiety of the gal "waiting for my man to come home" from the war, on this vocal by Peggy Lee in 1945. Peggy was on her own after leaving Goodman's band.

"Well, Git It!" - Ziggy Elman's trumpeting on this Sy Oliver arrangement for T. Dorsey is unforgettable. It's the best of Oliver's instrumentals with the band. And don't overlook Buddy Rich's talent on drums and Chuck Peterson backing Elman on trumpet.

"What Is This Thing Called Love?" - Shaw's lively version of this old classic uses strings to the best advantage backing vocalist Mel Torme. One of the best as the Velvet Fog laments, "I saw you there, one wonderful day. You took my heart and threw it away."

"Who Wouldn't Love You?" - It's Kyser time again with Trudy Erwin and Babbitt doing the vocal honors. The disc is lively, guaranteed to put the listener into a good mood while listening to the fine work of a well-coordinated sax section. When this record was cut - in 1942 - Kyser had earned 47 charted hits, 24 of them in the top 10. Trudy? She was the one with the Girl-Next-Door voice.

"You're Breaking My Heart" - Harry Prime sings with Flanagan's band - the group's first big hit. Vic Damone came along and did the same song in 1949. It was Damone's best-ever vocal. Damone could really sing. Take it from someone who knew - Sinatra.

Chapter 10

The Best

Just who were the best Big Band Era vocalists and recorded songs? Obviously, there's plenty of room for argument. Anybody's choices are, to be sure, strictly subjective.

For what it's worth, here are my selections - my subjective choices - following a careful examination (and enjoying it enormously) a select group of 200 separate recordings from the many thousands pressed during the Big Band Era:

BANDS

1. Artie Shaw
2. Benny Goodman
3. Tommy Dorsey
4. Harry James
5. Glenn Miller
6. Vaughn Monroe
7. Ralph Flanagan
8. Count Basie
9. Bob Wills (Yes, Wills)
10. Jimmie Lunceford

MALE VOCALISTS

1. Frank Sinatra
2. Vaughn Monroe
3. Ray Eberle
4. Dick Haymes
5. Nat "King" Cole

FEMALE VOCALISTS

1. Helen Forrest
2. Jo Stafford
3. Kitty Kallen
4. Anita O'Day
5. Bea Wain

BEST SONGS

1. "There's No You," Frank Sinatra backed by Axel Stordahl's studio band.
2. "True," Vaughn Monroe with vocals by Monroe and the 4 Lee Sisters.
3. "Well, Git It!", Tommy Dorsey instrumental,
4. "I Only Have Eyes For You," unknown studio band.
5. "Night and Day," Tommy Dorsey.
6. "It's Always You," Benny Goodman with vocal by Helen Forrest.
7. "The Trolley Song," Jo Stafford backed by Paul Weston's studio band.
8. "Darktown Strutter's Ball," Benny

Goodman.

9. "What Is This Thing Called Love?", Artie Shaw with vocal by Mel Torme.

10. "I Should Care," Ralph Flanagan with vocals by Harry Prime and the Singing Winds.

Chapter 11

Sinatra: A Class by Himself

Whatever he stirred, it wasn't motherly," moaned a former Bobby Soxer.

"That Sinatra hits those kids right in the kidney," complained a theatre usher.

The Frank Sinatra Story is not the sensational aspect of his personal life, it is what he contributed to the world of music, in particular, and to the world of entertainment, in general.

Sinatra (1915-1998), hailed by many as the

Entertainer of the Century, spent more than 50 years in show business.

Almost from the outset of his career in 1939, it was clear that Sinatra was an entirely new breed of singer. He possessed a rich, warm baritone voice with a relatively straight, unblemished delivery.

"Frank Sinatra is by any reasonable criterion the greatest singer in the history of popular music," wrote New York Times' music critic John Rockwell in his book, "Sinatra - An American Classic."

Rockwell accurately recalled how the excitement over Sinatra peaked at the Bobby Soxers' command center, Manhattan's Paramount Theatre, during the 1944 Columbus Day riot.

The theatre, said Rockwell, offered six or seven showings per day of a film, interspersed with Sinatra's appearance. There were 3,600 seats and the custom was that one could hold his or her seat as long as one stayed in it.

The girls would cling to their positions for hours and relieve themselves on the spot when necessary rather than relinquish their precious seats.

According to Rockwell, the most evocative recollection of what it was like to be a Bobby Soxer appeared in a 1974 edition of the New York Times (30 years after the fact).

Martha Weinman Lear lived in Boston at the time and gave vent to her adolescent longings. What she felt was shared by girls all over America.

"Frankie! we screamed from the balcony, the Bostonian recalled, "because you couldn't get an orchestra seat unless you were standing in line at dawn, and how could you explain to Mom that you were leaving for school before dawn?

"And that glorious sheltered spaghetti strand, down there in the spotlight, would croon on serenely, giving us a quick flick of a smile or, as a special bonus, a sidelong tremor of the lower lip.

"And then, the other thing: The voice had that trick, you know, that funny little sliding, skimming slur he would do coming off the end of a note. It drove us bonkers . . . it was an invitation to hysterics.

"We were sick all right, crazy."

Sinatra's notable intonation, beat and

spectacular phrasing were much admired by musicians, making him the finest crooner of the Big Band Era (1935-1946) and eventually the top male singer of the 20th century. Those who were privileged to see and hear him were touched by the quality, the integrity and good taste that provided most of his creative contributions to music forever.

Whenever Sinatra walked into a recording studio, night club or ballroom something electrical happened. Fellow musicians and fans both sensed it before he even began phrasing some of his incomparable hits.

Harry James signed Sinatra when he was singing at the Rustic Cabin in Englewood, N.J., in 1939. He next went with T. Dorsey.

I again refer you to Gunther Schuller, from "The Swing Era":

"Sinatra brought a new type of free and natural phrasing of songs, which not even Bing Crosby could match. Sensitivity, interpretive imagination, subtle jazz inflections and a fine beat, even on slow ballads, characterized Sinatra's crooning."

Schuller said that the newest feature of Sinatra's singing was the sheer quality of the voice itself.

"After decades of colorless, lightweight male voices, mostly effeminate-sounding tenors, Sinatra's virile, earthy baritone, with a rich voice, was a startling departure from the popular norm, observed Schuller.

Sinatra's million-seller hits, "I'll Never Smile Again" and "This Love of Mine," were musical breakthroughs imitated by hordes of other singers through the years.

Sinatra cut 84 sides for Dorsey, beginning in 1940 with "The Sky Fell Down" and ending in 1942 with "Light a Candle in the Chapel."

When he went out on his own, the initial enthusiasm for Sinatra soon bloomed into a national teenage love affair.

. . . And then in the 1950's some guy named Elvis electrified the teenage music world all over again and a whole new love affair was born. Uh, huh.

Chapter 12

December Song

End of the Trail

The body it crumbles, grace and vigor depart. There is now a stone where I once had a heart. But inside this old body, a young boy still dwells. And now and again my battered heart swells. I remember the joys and remember the pain, and I'm loving and living life over again on the Big Band dance floor. I think of the years, all too few, gone too fast.

And accept the stark fact that nothing can last. So open your eyes, youngsters, open and see, not a crabby old man, look closer, see me.

Anonymous (paraphrased)

Printed in the United States
1437800002BA/226